Ephesians: God's Plan and Our Response

By Rev. Cody Sandahl

Copyright ©2016 Cody Sandahl
All Rights Reserved.

Cover Photo by Norman Herr

No part of this book may be reproduced without the expressed written consent of the author except for the use of brief quotations in a book review or scholarly journal.

First Printing: 2016

ISBN 978-0692745151

Inquiries should be addressed to:
Rev. Cody Sandahl
codysandahl@gmail.com
www.codysandahl.com

Published by Azar Press in the United States of America

For chapter introduction videos, visit codysandahl.com/ephesians.

Table of Contents

Introduction 1
    MIND, HEART, AND BODY 2

Ephesians 1 4
    DEVOTIONAL 4
    GREETING (1:1-2) 5
    REMINDER AND ENCOURAGEMENT (1:3-14) 6
    THANKSGIVING AND PRAYER (1:15-23) 9

Ephesians 2 12
    DEVOTIONAL 12
    AMAZING GRACE (2:1-10) 13
    BREAKING DOWN THE WALL OF DIVISION (2:11-22) 18

Ephesians 3 23
    DEVOTIONAL 23
    THE MYSTERY REVEALED (3:1-13) 24
    THE FIRST ENDING PRAYER (3:14-21) 27

Ephesians 4 30
    DEVOTIONAL 30
    THE CHURCH'S UNITY AND MATURITY (4:1-16) 31
    LIVING INTO OUR SPIRITUAL MATURITY (4:17-32) 34

Ephesians 5 38
    DEVOTIONAL 38
    FROM DARKNESS TO LIGHT (5:1-20) 39
    THE CHRISTIAN FAMILY (5:21-33) 42

Ephesians 6 46
    DEVOTIONAL 46
    SERVE CHRIST, NOT PEOPLE (6:1-9) 47
    THE DAILY BATTLE (6:10-24) 50

Summary and Major Take-Aways 54

Background 56
    EPHESUS THE CITY 56

>   EPHESUS THE CHURCH 60
>   CONTEXT FOR THE LETTER 61
>   TIPS FOR READING 63
> **Using This Bible Study With a Small Group or Class 66**
> **References and Abbreviations..68**

Introduction

When I was in high school and college, it would have been mighty pleasant to be able to peek at the questions before the exam. I used to wish that my teacher or professor would line out the future exam questions along with the syllabus I received on the first day of class. I actually had a class in college that had take-home exams, and my initial glee was quickly subsumed under a self-imposed pressure. I would have gladly taken a 92 on the test, but since I had the time and ability and even invitation from the professor to check my answers before turning it in I felt I *had* to get a 100 on it. I might be a perfectionist at heart. When that professor gave us an option on the final – take-home or normal in-class exam – I actually chose the in-class exam so I wouldn't stress out as much about every single question.

Ephesians, with its birds-eye-view of God's story unfolding in Jesus' birth, life, teachings, crucifixion, resurrection, and promised return, is like having a take-home exam. Almost all of the essentials of the faith are found in this short book. Almost all of the ways we are to respond to our faith with our daily lives are found in this short book. If the hefty size of the Bible causes your mouth to suddenly dry up like the sands of the Mojave Desert, Ephesians is for you! It's like the Cliff's Notes version of the Bible.

But it is also a challenging book. As you read it, you may feel the same pressure I did in my college course – the pressure to be perfect. The pressure to get everything right in your life. The pressure to figure everything out. Ephesians has you covered, there, too. We are reminded that we are not saved by being perfect (thankfully):

> *it is by grace you have been saved, through faith—and this is not from yourselves, it is the gift of God—* ^{9} *not by works, so that no one can boast. – Ephesians 2:8-9 (NIV)*

In addition to its marvelously succinct approach to the sweeping arc of God's story, Ephesians also walks us through very earthly conversations as well. How should men and women interact with each other? How should children and parents interact with each other?

For those who like a good fight, there are controversies galore. If you want to take your life into your own hands, try quoting Ephesians

5:22 to my feminist mom: "wives be subject to your husbands..." (NIV). I have $20 on my mom if it comes to fisticuffs.

For those who are interested in social justice, Ephesians dives into slavery and power imbalances. We will explore the ups and downs of how Christians throughout the ages have attacked, defended, or accepted the practice of slavery.

For those who enter into spiritual battle through prayer, Ephesians contains some of the most strident depictions of evil and the devil. We are assumed to be under attack at all times, but the author also shows us the way out.

The book of Ephesians has something for everyone. From the big picture to the day-to-day. From exaltation in Christ to opposition by the devil. From encouragement to challenge. My prayers go with you as you grow closer to Christ through the letter to the church in Ephesus.

Mind, Heart, and Body

In addition to the chapter-by-chapter analysis of Ephesians, I have also included a Personal Devotional at the start of each chapter. We are encouraged to "be transformed by the renewing of your mind" (Romans 12:2 NIV), but we are also reminded that God "will give you a new heart and put a new spirit in you" (Ezekiel 36:26a NIV). Our spiritual growth involves our minds and our hearts. The personal devotionals are designed to reach the heart since the Bible study reaches the mind.

If you are walking through Ephesians with a small group or Bible study, the devotionals are also there for you if you are running out of time this week and just have five minutes before the group gathers. Don't worry – I won't tell anyone. This study is flexible enough to be anywhere from six to fourteen weeks long. You can find a week-by-week guide listing the suggested reading plans near the end of this book.

On the other end of the spectrum, if you are a history buff or a church history wonk or a Bible trivia collector, first let me greet you as a brother or sister. We have so much in common! If you also like Star Wars we should meet – we'll be fast friends. At the end of this book (in the Background section) you will find information about the city of Ephesus, the church in Ephesus, and how Ephesus plays a major role in the unfolding of God's story after Jesus' ascension to heaven. If you want to know how archeology, prostitution, and the Word of God interact with each other in Ephesus, check out the Background section.

Hopefully this book will help you grow closer to Christ whether you have five minutes or five hours this week to contemplate the book of Ephesians.

Ephesians 1

Devotional

As I read Paul's opening to his letter to the church in Ephesus, I am struck by how often he mentions blessings and reasons to give thanks to God. He starts off with the blessings and thanksgivings that apply to every Christian. God "blessed us in Christ with every spiritual blessing in the heavenly places" (v3). He highlights the "good pleasure of his will" (v5) and gives "praise of his glorious grace that he freely bestowed on us" (v6). Paul celebrates "the riches of his grace that he lavished on us" (v7-8). We have an "inheritance" in Christ (v11, 14) and so we have "hope" (v12).

Then he moves on to the special ways God has blessed and worked through the church in Ephesus. They are famous for their "faith in the Lord Jesus and your love toward all the saints" (v15). Paul is praying for them constantly (v16). God has the power to work in them and through them (v19-20). And lest anyone think their problem is too big for God, Paul reminds them that God "has put all things under his feet and has made him the head over all things for the church" (v22).

I don't know about you, but I often find it all too easy to focus on my reasons to complain rather than my litany of blessings. As I write this, I am staring out a window as a light rain transforms into a heavy rain/snow mix. Gotta love mountain weather. I'm going to leave and get into my car in a few minutes. Oh, and I also forgot my coat. My first thought was somewhat less than thankful toward the provision of this precipitation. But as a neighbor recently reminded me, "at least we won't have to worry about water this year." One person's annoying rain or snow is another person's gift of life-giving water. The difference is our perspective.

GOING DEEPER

- What are the blessings and thanksgivings you can think of that every human or every Christian or even every American should remember?
- What are the special blessings and thanksgivings God has placed in your life?
- Is there some part of your life that could use a switch to a thankful perspective?

- Paul was continually praying for others – even people he had never personally met. Where might God be calling you to expand your prayer this week to include new people or situations?

Greeting (1:1-2)

Most letters from Paul start off with a simple greeting that reminds people who he is (an apostle sent by Christ) and offers them a short blessing. As with many of the letters, in Ephesians he offers "grace and peace." In short, this amounts to saying, "I hope you can see God at work in your lives, and I hope that gives you a calmness about your present and your future." More information is contained in the Background section, but this letter may be written by Paul or someone later on who invoked Paul's name to indicate they were claiming his teaching and theology as their influence. Also, this letter may be written to several churches in Asia Minor rather than just the church in Ephesus.

While Ephesians starts off very similarly to other letters from Paul, it begins to diverge immediately by what follows the greeting. Usually Paul acknowledges some problem in the church pretty early on. In Galatians, for instance, he says by verse 6, "I am astonished that you are so quickly deserting the one who called you to live in the grace of Christ and are turning to a different gospel—which is really no gospel at all. Evidently some people are throwing you into confusion and are trying to pervert the gospel of Christ" (Galatians 1:6-7 NIV). By contrast, the entire first chapter of Ephesians is centered on blessing and thanksgiving.

If your Bible has section titles, it is useful to know that those section titles were added by the translators rather than being present in the original manuscripts. Sometimes those section titles are difficult to place. In this case they are rather straightforward, because verses 3-14 are a single long Greek sentence and verses 15-23 are another long Greek sentence. English translations split these verses into multiple sentences because the English language isn't built for sentences like these.

Reminder and Encouragement (1:3-14)

In my family, as in many families, whenever we all get together we tell stories. I find it interesting that we keep telling the same stories every time we get the chance, with a few new ones thrown in for good measure. It fascinates me that these stories are told repeatedly despite everyone in the room already knowing the entire story. If there's a funny joke, everyone already knows the punch line. If there's an embarrassing moment, surely the embarrassment has faded over the years of retelling. And yet we keep telling the same stories. Why?

Pamela Rutledge writes in an article for Psychology Today that stories are how we make sense of our experiences [WEB1]. She writes, "Stories are how we think. They are how we make meaning of life...how we understand our place in the world, create our identities, and define and teach social values." In other words, stories are how we know who we are. At family gatherings and high school reunions and really any place that humans repeatedly gather, we tell stories to remind ourselves who we are.

Hendrik Kraemer was a Dutch missionary to Indonesia during World War II [WEB2]. One night as he was home he was approached by some fellow Christians who asked him what they should do now that the Gestapo was rounding up their Jewish neighbors. Ronald J. Greer tells what happened next:

> *And Hendrik Kraemer said to them, "I am not going to tell you what to do, but I will tell you who you are. And if you know who you are, then you will know what to do." He opened his Bible to 1 Peter and began to read: "You are a chosen race, a royal priesthood, a dedicated nation, and a people claimed by God as his own, to proclaim the triumphs of Him who has called you out of darkness and into his marvelous light." Dr. Kraemer closed his Bible. "Do you know who you are?" he asked, "Then you'll know what to do." Thanking him, the group left his house. That night, they formed the Dutch Resistance. – "If You Know Who You Are You Will Know What to Do"*

This section of Ephesians is re-telling the story of Jesus, not because they didn't know it but precisely because they already did. This re-telling is designed to remind the church who they are so that (later in the letter) they will know what to do.

There are three key points – three touchstones – that we are to remember through this re-telling of the story. First, the writer reminds us again and again that **God has had a plan forever and he's making it happen**. For example, we see that "in love he predestined us" (1:5 NIV), "he purposed in Christ" (1:9 NIV), and especially "in him we were also chosen, having been predestined according to the plan of him who works out everything in conformity with the purpose of his will" (1:11 NIV).

The Greek word for "predestine" is a rarely used [KIT] form of a word that means "boundary" or "territory" or "limit." So the image is of God setting out the limits of Creation before light ever shone on the Earth. Importantly, this word is used in Scripture (Acts 4:28, Romans 8:29-30) to talk about God's salvation plan rather than controlling our everyday activities. This is about God planning our eternal destination rather than planning our lunch menu.

It is also important to note the tone with which the author speaks of this eternal plan. Notice how it starts with "blessing" in v3 and continues to talk about "praise" and "glory" (v12, 14). This eternal plan is something to celebrate, not something to fear. Now that we know we are part of God's eternal plan, we are encouraged to be grateful and be at peace.

The second touchstone is to remember that **we are adopted into God's family because Jesus chose to make us his sisters and brothers** (v5). Do you know anyone who has done an international adoption? Many times the adopting families have to wait for over a year before they get the call to fly over and meet their new child, and that means they are signing up to adopt someone who hasn't even been conceived yet. The child's parents aren't known yet, so they aren't being chosen for their pedigree. The child hasn't been born so it hasn't done anything to deserve special treatment. The simple fact that the child *will be born someday* is enough for some families to choose to adopt.

The author writes that this adoption is "in accordance with his pleasure and will" (v5 NIV), and "freely given" (v6 NIV). In other words, we bring as much to the table as the unborn child for those families in international adoption. We have no desirable birthright. We have no track record of impressive actions – actually we have a long track record of unimpressive actions, so that baby has a leg up on us! This adoption into God's family is totally a result of the action of God.

As a result of this adoption, we have "redemption through his blood, the forgiveness of sins, in accordance with the riches of God's grace that he lavished on us" (v7-8a NIV). Because we are family, we are bailed out of jail. Because we are family, we are forgiven for everything we've done or will do. Because we are family, God grants us an "inheritance" (v14 NIV) of eternal salvation. We are children of God because we are brothers and sisters of Jesus.

The third touchstone is that we are **"marked in him with a seal, the promised Holy Spirit"** (v13 NIV). If you have ever watched a movie that takes place in ancient times, you have surely seen a king use his ring to imprint his sign on the wax seal of a letter. This was designed to provide security (opening the letter breaks the seal) and to indicate ownership of the contents (who said these words) [ARCH].

To be marked with the seal of the Holy Spirit is to be claimed by God and to be protected by God. Jesus says of the Holy Spirit, "And I will ask the Father, and he will give you another advocate to help you and be with you forever" (John 14:16 NIV), and "But the Advocate, the Holy Spirit, whom the Father will send in my name, will teach you all things and will remind you of everything I have said to you" (John 14:26 NIV). In other words, God is personally present in our lives through the Holy Spirit. This presence takes the promises enumerated in Ephesians 1:3-14 and makes them active in our lives.

GOING DEEPER

- God's plan has been in the works for thousands of years, but it hasn't come to full fruition yet. How do you feel knowing that God is in control? How do you feel when you see the gulf between where we are and what God promises to eventually be true?
- The letter to the Ephesians says you are an adopted child of God. How do you normally identify yourself? What are the important parts of your identity? How does being a "child of God" alter or reinforce your identity?
- How do you imagine or relate to the Holy Spirit? When have you felt the nearness of the Holy Spirit? When have you wondered where the Holy Spirit was hiding?

- Now that you know who you are, is there anything God wants you to do?

Thanksgiving and Prayer (1:15-23)

When you watch or read the news, how does it make you feel about the human race? How many of the articles make you want to smile and cheer? I imagine that Paul felt that head-slapping sense of "now what?" that we sometimes feel reading the news. After all, if things were going swimmingly in all the churches he helped start, we wouldn't have so many letters from Paul in the New Testament!

With that backdrop in mind, I imagine it was kind of nice to be able to write "ever since I heard about your faith in the Lord Jesus and your love for all God's people, **I have not stopped giving thanks for you**" (1:15-16a NIV). It is important to note the headlines to this piece of good news: "faith…and love." If you compare this with other letters from Paul, you will see that many of the issues in the churches arise from a lack of faith or a lack of love. It is good news when our faith leads us to love. It is bad news when we miss one of those steps.

These verses also give us a **powerful prayer pattern** for our own lives. We first see thanksgiving. Then we see that prayer is a regular task, not an occasional diversion (v16). The author also praises God for who he is, not just what he can do for us (v16). In a similar vein, he prays for a closer relationship with God for its own sake (v16). Only after these other prayers does the author move into his specific prayers for the people of the church. This prayer pattern is reminiscent of the Lord's Prayer in Matthew 6:9-13 and Luke 11:1-4.

Once the author moves into the specific prayers for the church, the focus shifts to **God's power** (v19ff). The Greek word for "power" essentially means "to be able" [MOU]. The author says, "incomparably great power" (v19), "mighty strength" (v19), "far above all rule and authority" (v21), "power and dominion" (v21), "all things under his feet" (v22), "head over everything" (v22). We can probably infer from these repeated reminders of God's abilities that the hearers had some doubts on that front. We know that many of the local religions in Asia Minor acknowledged malicious and capricious gods who approached humans with the same affection as a child using a magnifying glass in the sun to burn ants on the ground [APOL]. Perhaps the early Christian converts had yet to fully shed their religious upbringing. Or perhaps they had transferred over to Jesus some of the malicious qualities of their former gods and they were walking on eggshells afraid of the next thunderbolt from the smiting God.

These verses mark the beginning of a theme of spiritual warfare [JNTC] that will be taken up later in the other chapters in Ephesians. A friend of mine once told me a story of being an RA on his floor in the college dorm. Something terrible had happened and so the RA's were tasked with cleaning out this student's room. As he walked in he felt a sense of evil pervading the space that was as thick as molasses. If you have never had an experience such as this, you might think that people who talk about spiritual warfare are nuts. But if you have ever been in the presence of tangible evil, you know all too well what they are talking about. The letter to the Ephesians acknowledges this spiritual reality that is intertwined with but also somewhat different than the physical reality we see in front of us. The author of this letter is battling on behalf of the church through prayer.

Finally, the last two verses of chapter one remind us that **Christ is the summary of God's whole plan**. Verse 22 is partially a quote of Psalm 110:1 – "Lord says to my lord: 'Sit at my right hand until I make your enemies a footstool for your feet'" (NIV). While we no longer have such positions of authority, in ancient times the person who sat at the right hand of the king had the authority to act on behalf of the king. In fact, in Scripture the right hand of God is known as a position of favor (Psalm 80:18), victory (Isaiah 41:10), and power (Exodus 15:6) [WORD].

The second part of v22 talks about Christ as the head over all things. This is kind of like saying, "that person has a good head on their shoulders." Head in this context is a summing up of the whole person, not just their intellect. Similarly, when the author writes that Christ is the "head over all things" he's implying that God's whole purpose and character are summed up in Christ. Do you want to know what God's plan is? Get to know Jesus. Do you want to know who God is? Get to know Jesus. This was actually a strong statement that ran against one of the insurgency movements in early Christianity. Gnostics believed that a second revelation of special, hidden knowledge was needed to truly know God. If Christ is the summing up of God's will and plan and purpose, there isn't any hidden knowledge. It's there for anyone to see.

Verse 23 takes this idea of Christ as the summing up of God's plan and purpose and then applies it to the church. Christ is the head but the church is the body. That means Jesus chooses to work through us. It is

God's plan to call and equip the saints for the work of ministry (Ephesians 4:12) rather than making everything happen without us.

GOING DEEPER

- Knowing that God is able to do anything can be both an incredible comfort but also a stumbling block. When has God's power comforted you in times of trial? When has God's lack of action caused you to doubt or question who God is?
- Looking at v15-16, how do your own prayers line up or diverge from the prayer pattern? Another common prayer pattern is ACTS: Adoration, Confession, Thanksgiving, Supplication. Which of those prayers are natural for you, and which require discipline?
- Jesus chooses to make the church his body in the world. When has God worked through someone else to reach you? When has God worked through you? How do you think God wants to work through your church as the local body of Christ?

Ephesians 2

Devotional

When I was growing up I always thought it was entertaining to watch the commercials for diets, exercises, dermatology, and the like. They always had the "before" and "after" pictures to show how amazing their product could be. I had to laugh, though, because the "before" picture was usually in bad lighting and was always, without fail, a picture of the person frowning. And the "after" picture was always, without fail, a picture of the person smiling in great lighting with probably a professional photographer arranging the most flattering pose.

Similarly, Pepsi ran a very successful campaign where they did blindfolded taste testing between Pepsi and Coca-Cola. When they didn't know what they were drinking, people chose Pepsi most of the time. But rumors persist that Pepsi was served at a refreshingly chilled temperature whereas the Coke was served slightly warm.

In both instances, companies are trying to make their product look better than it is by rigging the comparison. I was reminded of these stories as I read Paul's words starting in v11. He starts off with his "before" picture by asking them to "remember when…" And then in v13 he gives the "after" picture by telling them, "But now in Christ Jesus…" In v19 he says that before Christ you were "strangers and aliens," but now you are "citizens with the saints and also members of the household of God." That's an even bigger transformation than the latest diet or the amazing ShamWow or the incomparable OxiClean!

This passage actually used to trouble me quite a bit, because I didn't see that amazing "before" and "after" picture when I looked at my life. I grew up a Christian child of Christian parents. I knew Jesus loved me almost before I knew about Star Wars (almost). I didn't think I had a story of transformation. But then a friend of mine told me to think about it differently. Since I couldn't remember anything before knowing Jesus, instead she encouraged me to think about a time before I committed my life to Jesus. What did my life look like when Jesus was my copilot? And what did life look like when I swapped seats and let Jesus fly the plane? That's a story that actually has some "before" and "after." And unlike the commercials, I don't have to rig the comparison to see that following Jesus has made a tremendous impact on my life.

GOING DEEPER

- What's your "before" and "after" when it comes to Jesus? Do you have an easy comparison or do you have to look more closely as I did?
- What's one way that your faith has improved your life?
- What's one way that your faith has been challenging?
- Imagine that you had thirty seconds (60 words) to pitch Jesus to someone. What's your pitch?

Amazing Grace (2:1-10)

This section essentially communicates three things: non-Jews had no hope (2:1-3), but thanks to Jesus the free gift of salvation became available to everyone (2:4-9), so we can live in a new and God-honoring way (2:10). Let's take each of these in turn.

Non-Jews Had No Hope (2:1-3). The dominant image of these verses is of a person walking down a path (v2). The path laid out by the Adversary (called "the ruler of the kingdom of the air") looks wide and paved and easy, so we take it every chance we get. As Jesus said in Matthew:

> *13 "Enter through the narrow gate. For wide is the gate and broad is the road that leads to destruction, and many enter through it. 14 But small is the gate and narrow the road that leads to life, and only a few find it." – Matthew 7:13-14 (NIV)*

Figure 1. The Flammarion, artist unknown

It is important to spend a little bit of time unpacking this "ruler of the kingdom of the air" or the Adversary as I will refer to it. There is an assumption in many parts of the Bible that there is an oppositional force that actively works against God's will. For instance, Job 1 mentions **"Satan" which means Adversary** [VINE]. The most-known reference is probably Genesis 3, where the "serpent" was "crafty" and sowed doubt in the minds of Adam and Eve. In Revelation 12 and 20 the serpent is connected with the term "devil" which means "false accuser" or "slanderer" [VINE]. In Matthew 4, Jesus is tempted by the "devil" in the wilderness. Most interestingly in Matthew 4, the "devil" claims to have authority over the nations of the earth. It is somewhat unclear what this oppositional force is, but there are some important points. First, we see in Jesus' resurrection and in the book of Revelation that God wins. Whatever or whomever opposes God, they are unequal to God. Second, the temptation of Jesus implies that this force is external. Jesus never sinned, so the temptation could not have come from inside himself. That means that evil is not just an outgrowth of human impulses, but instead there is some sense of evil that adds extra pressure from the outside. Finally, we see in John 8:44 that "there is no truth" in the Adversary. All it has are lies. Jesus is the truth that overcomes the lies of the Adversary.

As an aside, there are various statements in Scripture that see some kind of spiritual hierarchy in the cosmos. In addition to v2 calling the Adversary "the ruler of the kingdom of the air," we have Paul saying in 2 Corinthians 12:2 that he knew a man caught up to the third heaven, and we see some kind of firmament that divides waters above and below in Genesis 1:6-8. You can see in the accompanying image an artist's conception of the structure of the universe, with the ground, the air, the "heavens" (stars), and then several levels of heaven above that. Using this image, we see that "ruler of the kingdom of the air" is in reference to the Adversary being thrown out of heaven (Revelation 12:7-12). The "kingdom of the air" is the last worldly zone before crossing into "the heavens." It is the glass ceiling the Adversary bumps into as he tries to take God's place (Isaiah 14:13). The writer's main point seems to be that we are unable to resist the Adversary, because it has more power than we do. This is especially true for Gentile Christians, as many Jews thought of the Adversary as controlling all the nations outside of Israel [IVP].

The Free Gift of Salvation Offered to All (2:4-9). From our Christian perspective, it's easy to think of the Law as something that had to be followed exactly for someone to earn salvation. We often think it was all about what a person had done. But we know that God saved the Jewish people before giving them the Law. For instance, God reminds them of how he already saved them when he gave them the Ten Commandments:

> *And God spoke all these words: ² "I am the Lord your God, who brought you out of Egypt, out of the land of slavery. ³ "You shall have no other gods before me. – Exodus 20:1-3 (NIV)*

Similarly, when God made his covenant with Abraham in Genesis 17, it was offered with circumcision as the only stipulation. God has been a God of grace since the very beginning. Jesus' crucifixion and resurrection are the prime examples of this character trait of God, and it's also the best way we know that God extended this blessing beyond the Jewish people, but it's not a unique event in God's plan to redeem us.

So while God's graciousness despite our unworthiness is a very old idea, Christianity did contain a new expectation that has no clear antecedent in the Old Testament. The contrast between personal "death" in the hopelessness of the past (v1) and the "made alive" hope of the present (v5) is a new pattern. Usually salvation in the Old Testament refers to the whole people of Israel, but here the writer makes a clear expectation of personal transformation [WORD]. If you've ever heard speakers at Christian events tell their stories, you've probably heard many variations on the "back then...but now" conversion story. I've heard about people going from drug addict to pastor, from abusive to peacemaker, from apathetic to activist. We're used to these stories, but at the time this letter was written that was a novel concept.

The clearest comparison we could make would be with the followers of the philosophers in the Greco-Roman context. To become a follower of a particular philosopher, a person often had to swear an oath to follow the core tenets [WEB3]. There was a clear expectation of transformation, but it was a result of your mind and your actions. You had to earn the right to call yourself a member of a particular philosophical school.

Contrast that with what is written here in Ephesians:

> *it is by grace you have been saved, through faith—and this is not from yourselves, it is the gift of God—* ⁹ *not by works, so that no one can boast.* – Ephesians 2:8-9 (NIV)

This is one of the most unique and shocking claims of Christianity. We don't have to earn our way. In fact, since we *can't* earn our way that is incredibly good news! I'm not an expert in world religions by any means, but as I look at most of the other approaches to faith I see very few examples of such freely offered grace. This is actually one of the verses where the Bible as we know it differs from the Book of Mormon, which adds a requirement of good deeds:

> *"For we know that it is by grace that we have been saved, <u>after all we do</u>"* – 2 Nephi 25:23, *emphasis added* [APOL]

I believe it is also worth noting that the Greek word for "grace" was mainly used as an aesthetic observation [WORD]. When I was in seminary we had an annual flag football game against another seminary that was just down the road. While we were practicing, I caught a pass, spun away from a defender, and sprinted into the end zone. A teammate used the word "graceful" to describe the play. Surely that had everything to do with natural ability and nothing to do with being twenty years younger than the defender. Okay, maybe a better example from my seminary days comes from our talent show. One of my friends was a professional dancer before entering ministry, and his performances put my "graceful" football play to shame.

My dancer friend is a perfect example of why the word "grace" is used here and elsewhere in the New Testament. My friend simply carried himself in such a way that exuded poise and grace. He was so aware of and in control of his body that you could just tell he was different. He *walked* with grace. He *sat* with grace. He was noticeably different at any given moment, even if you couldn't put your finger on the reason why. That's what the writer is trying to connote by using the word "grace." We are given a free and inexplicable gift, and as a result something is different about us even as we walk around the room.

Living in a God-Honoring Way (2:10). Continuing that image of grace, we are described as God's "handiwork." The Greek word is an image of a craftsman carefully weaving or carving. It is an image of an artist ignoring distractions as she carefully and competently brushes on the paint *just so*. Two summers ago I was joined by a friend in building a CNC mill in my basement. This is basically a robotic tool that carves a 3D plan into a piece of wood, foam, etc. If your machine is off by even a little bit, your final carving is going to show it. My friend and I had to carefully measure every dimension, double-check each part, and tune it to a tenth of a millimeter. When it was finally completed, I was a wee bit perturbed that we had a wobble whenever the carver was moved in a particular direction. I discovered that we had misplaced a single part. Even though it was only one millimeter thick, that was enough to throw off the carving. And yes, Murphy's Law struck again and I had to disassemble half of the machine to replace this one stupid part. Even though I was muttering in a non-pastorly way as I went, I took everything apart, placed the washer in the right place, reassembled everything, and carefully re-tuned the carver. That's the kind of care God takes in crafting us.

The CNC mill is just a giant paperweight unless it has a job to do. It is a tool. It is a means to an end. It allows me to make other things. Similarly, God took care in crafting us for a purpose. We aren't saved by our good works, but we are saved *for* good works. God crafted us to be tools in this world. We, like the robotic carver, have jobs to do.

GOING DEEPER

- The first section (2:1-3) implies that we face a kind of gravity pulling us away from God due to the Adversary working in the world. How much do you feel that pull away from God's path? Do you find it easier to see God's path when you're on it or when you're far away from it?
- How do you think about the Adversary?
- Do you find yourself trying to earn God's grace?
- Who have you known that exuded the "grace" of God as my dancer friend exuded physical grace?
- Why has God carefully crafted you? What has God already done through you? What do you think God wants to do through you now or in the future?

Breaking Down the Wall of Division (2:11-22)

Sometimes these verses are used by Christians to justify a sense of superiority over the Jews. Ironically, the context was the exact opposite at the time. Paul constantly battled against "Judaizers" who told the Gentiles that they needed to be circumcised and follow kosher rules to be real Christians (Galatians 2, Acts 15). They thought that those who were circumcised had reason to boast over those who were not. I find it more likely that the writer spent twelve verses talking about reconciliation and unity so that we can relate with others on equal, not superior, footing.

This attitude can even be present within Christianity. In a conversation about the differences between Christianity in Europe and the USA versus China, Africa, and South America, I once heard someone say that our interpretations of Scripture are better because we are so much more educated about the Bible. The assumption was that we know so much we can escape our cultural biases whereas pastors elsewhere are trapped by their cultural heritage. My highly technical response was, "Yikes! I'm not with you on that one."

Let's unpack the imagery in this section and see where it leads us. The **first image is "citizenship in Israel" (v12)**. The Greek word there is the root from which we get "politics." It implies membership, citizenship, and corporate life together [JNTC]. It serves as a reminder that God's story of salvation goes through Israel. We as Gentile Christians are granted spiritual citizenship with Israel as part of God's salvation story. Paul directly addresses this in Romans 11 when he tells Gentile Christians that they are an offshoot of Israel's branch:

> *17 If some of the branches have been broken off, and you, though a wild olive shoot, have been grafted in among the others and now share in the nourishing sap from the olive root, 18 do not consider yourself to be superior to those other branches. If you do, consider this: You do not support the root, but the root supports you. – Romans 11:17-18 (NIV)*

Whenever I watch the Olympics, I suddenly care about curling and even speed walking because some people have USA on their jersey. Why? Because they are fellow citizens of my country. In a like manner we are to cheer for our Jewish brothers and sisters because we are in some sense on the same team. There are plenty of times in Scripture where the Jewish people aren't following God's commands (like almost all of the Old Testament), so it's not a *carte blanche* stamp upon the policies of the *nation* of Israel, but we are still supposed to see ourselves on the same team rather than in opposition to each other.

The **next image is the "dividing wall of hostility" between Jews and Gentiles**. This is a reference to a series of pillars that were erected inside the Temple complex to separate the Court of the Gentiles from Inner Court [ARCH]. These pillars had inscriptions in multiple languages warning non-Jews that they weren't permitted to go closer to the Temple. Archaeologists have actually discovered two of these, and they state, "No foreigner is allowed to enter within the balustrade surrounding the sanctuary and the court. Whoever is caught will be personally responsible for his ensuing death." They weren't messing around! In fact, when Paul was arrested and beaten in Acts 21:16-30 it was on the grounds that he supposedly brought in a Gentile to the Inner Court.

Interestingly, the Temple wasn't originally built with this dividing wall [ARCH]. For instance, 1 Kings 8 assumes that foreigners will come and pray at the Temple because they have heard of God's great name:

> *41 "As for the foreigner who does not belong to your people Israel but has come from a distant land because of your name— 42 for they will hear of your great name and your mighty hand and your outstretched arm—when they come and pray toward this temple, 43 then hear from heaven, your dwelling place. Do whatever the foreigner asks of you, so that all the peoples of the earth may know your name and fear you, as do your own people Israel, and may know that this house I have built bears your Name. –* 1 Kings 8:41-43 (NIV)

There are similar divisions even today. When I went to the Wailing Wall, there was a divider separating the men and women. I will point out, however, that a *bar mitzvah* was taking place while I was there and they had the celebration at the barrier so the men and women on both sides of the wall could participate together. There is also another covered section that has been the subject of considerable debate about who can use it.

I believe the author is primarily trying to show that, through Jesus, God has eliminated the difference in his approach to Jews and Gentiles. Previously God had singled out the Jewish people to be the caretakers of his Word and to be an example to the Gentiles. Now God is interacting with all people directly, thus eliminating the wall of distinction and the pride of place.

It is important to note, however, that Jesus did not destroy the Jewish Law itself. Jesus himself said in Matthew 5:

> *"Do not think that I have come to abolish the Law or the Prophets; I have not come to abolish them but to fulfill them. 18 For truly I tell you, until heaven and earth disappear, not the smallest letter, not the least stroke of a pen, will by any means disappear from the Law until everything is accomplished." –* Matthew 5:17-18 (NIV)

Right after Jesus said those words he changed the focus, emphasis, and priority of the Law in the Sermon on the Mount (Matthew 5-7), but he did not eliminate it. If anything, the Sermon on the Mount intensified the Law rather than wiping it off the books. As Christians, we can't ignore the Old Testament. We should always look to see if Jesus changed the trajectory or meaning or importance of something from the Old Testament, but we can't ignore it.

The **final image sees the church as being built into a new "holy temple in the Lord" (v21)**. This is a common image in the New Testament letters. 1 Peter 2 expands this further:

> *[4] As you come to him, the living Stone—rejected by humans but chosen by God and precious to him— [5] you also, like living stones, are being built into a spiritual house to be a holy priesthood, offering spiritual sacrifices acceptable to God through Jesus Christ. [6] For in Scripture it says: "See, I lay a stone in Zion, a chosen and precious cornerstone, and the one who trusts in him will never be put to shame." – 1 Peter 2:4-6 (NIV)*

Another twist on this image sees each individual Christian as a temple:

> *[19] Do you not know that your bodies are temples of the Holy Spirit, who is in you, whom you have received from God? You are not your own; [20] you were bought at a price. Therefore honor God with your bodies. – 1 Corinthians 6:19-20 (NIV)*

Notice the tense of the words in Ephesians and 1 Peter. In both we are "being built" rather than "already built." We as the Church and we as individual Christians have "under construction" signs hanging prominently from our lives. We are "[rising] to become a holy temple" (v21), but we aren't there yet. I, for one, am quite grateful that Paul and Peter chose to use ongoing tenses rather than finished tenses, because I'm certainly not a holy temple of the Holy Spirit yet.

GOING DEEPER

- How do you see your relationship with followers of the Jewish faith? What about the modern-day nation of Israel?
- What "dividing walls of hostility" do you see still standing today? Are there any such walls that you are especially passionate about? If so, what role do you see the church playing in reinforcing or tearing down that wall?
- How has God already done some construction in your life? What parts of your life are actively under construction right now?

Ephesians 3

Devotional

When I was in middle school, I loved going on long car rides with my dad, because he always had the best books on tape (yes, tape). From Clive Cussler novels to old radio dramas, my dad had it all. One of my favorites was *The Shadow* from the 1930's. "Who knows what evil lurks in the hearts of men? The Shadow knows!" The Shadow could speak any language, solve any puzzle, and even cloud men's minds.

As I read this third chapter of Paul's letter, I'm reminded of that slogan because Paul bounces between what we know to be true and what isn't known, except maybe to The Shadow. He lifts up the "mystery of Christ" (v3-5, 9) four different times. Think about that. Even Paul, the great missionary, someone who was personally converted to the faith by a vision of the risen Christ, had to acknowledge that mystery remained in his faith. He didn't understand everything! If Paul couldn't figure some of these things out, maybe we shouldn't be surprised if we still have questions, too. In fact, maybe we should consider it a warning sign if we think we have everything figured out.

But on the other hand, Paul didn't regard his faith as just a mystery. He knew beyond a shadow of a doubt that we are saved by Jesus Christ (v5-6). He knew beyond a shadow of a doubt that God called him to proclaim this Gospel (v7). He knew beyond a shadow of a doubt that Jesus came to save not just the Jews but the Gentiles, too (v6, 8). He knew beyond a shadow of a doubt that God's plan was being worked out in the world (v11). He knew beyond a shadow of a doubt that we have reason for hope even if we're suffering right now (v13).

Some parts of our faith are unquestionably true. Other parts of our faith are still mysteries to be worked out.

GOING DEEPER

- What aspects of your faith seem rock-solid to you?
- What aspects of your faith still have questions marks or seem mysterious to you?
- If you could ask Jesus to explain one thing, what would you want to know?
- Where do you or someone you know need to pray in hope and not lose heart (v13)?

The Mystery Revealed (3:1-13)

As I'm writing this, I'm eavesdropping (Jesus please forgive me) on two Christian missionaries who are talking about the meaning of the following passage from Paul's letter to the church in Philippi:

> *10 I want to know Christ—yes, to know the power of his resurrection and participation in his sufferings, becoming like him in his death, 11 and so, somehow, attaining to the resurrection from the dead. – Philippians 3:10-11 (NIV)*

Their conclusion is that the only way to truly know the heart of Christ is to suffer with him and for him and on his behalf. This is an interesting part of Paul's message. If you put together your resume for a job interview, are you going to proudly highlight your failures and firings and shortcomings? When a politician gives a stump speech, do they lead off with the ways they were unable to fulfill their campaign promises? When an athlete is introduced at an event, do we list their injuries and the times they missed or stumbled or fell? Of course not! But Paul routinely uses his suffering as a marker of his authority and a way of identifying with Jesus.

Here the Ephesians are reminded that Paul was imprisoned multiple times because of his ministry (v1), he is "less than the least of all the Lord's people" because he persecuted and killed Christians before his conversion (v8), that his entire ministry is a result of God's grace rather than his own ability (v2), and that he suffers on behalf of the churches he helped start (v13). **One of the mysteries of the gospel is that God works through our weakness and uses our failures and stands with us in our suffering to draw us closer to him.**

When I was at the beginning of my ministry as a pastor, I was well aware that I had lived a life that had more than its fair share of blessings. I worried that I couldn't be a complete pastor without someday experiencing deep or prolonged suffering – to "participate in [Christ's] sufferings." Now that I have experienced some level of suffering through our ongoing, years-long battle with my son's intractable seizures, I can definitely say I have been drawn closer to Christ. I have a larger heart for compassion. I understand how to avoid many of the common unhelpful things people say to those who are suffering. I have experienced complete reliance on God because we have run into the limits of human knowledge and power. I have been drawn closer to Christ.

I also find it interesting that **Paul's ministry is seated in the grand story of God's great plan** (v7-9). Daniel Pink, in his book *Drive: The Surprising Truth About What Motivates Us*, says that humans need three things to feel fully engaged and motivated: autonomy, mastery, and purpose. These verses highlight the immense purpose behind Paul's ministry and by extension our ministry. By taking on the role "to preach to the Gentiles," he played a part in God's timeless plan. Similarly, the writer encourages the Ephesians in v13 "not to be discouraged" because they are part of that grand story, too.

Looking back from our vantage point almost two thousand years later, we can see that most of the churches Paul started no longer exist. We can acknowledge that, while many of his letters were incorporated into the New Testament, that was primarily because the churches he helped start kept going off the deep end and needed correction! But his role in telling the good news about Jesus Christ to Gentiles (not just Jews) helped to start a movement that continues even today. On the day the church was started, there were about three thousand Christians, all of whom lived in Israel (Acts 2). Within the first century, there were approximately a million Christians living all over the Roman Empire [WEB4]. By 1910, there were about 600 million Christians, with 93% living in Europe or the Americas. In 2010, there were 2.1 billion Christians, spread between Europe (26%), the Americas (37%), Sub-Saharan Africa (24%), and the Asia-Pacific region (13%) [WEB5].

From a narrow view, Paul helped start a handful of the earliest churches and he helped to establish the idea that Jesus saves Jews and Gentiles. From a broader perspective, Paul's pebble that expanded the sharing of the Good News turned into an avalanche that continues to gather strength today. One man's death and resurrection in Israel is now the professed hope of a third of the people in the world. We, like the Ephesians, are encouraged to see our small role from a broader perspective, because God is creating mighty avalanches from our small pebbles rolling down the hill.

One final note on v2-6. The author writes that the mystery of how in Christ God brought the Gentiles into the promise of salvation "was not made known to people in other generations as it has now been revealed by the Spirit" (v5). There were definitely hints in the Old Testament that God was going to do something to save other nations. For instance, in Isaiah 19:25 God says:

> *The Lord Almighty will bless them, saying, "Blessed be Egypt my people, Assyria my handiwork, and Israel my inheritance." – Isaiah 19:25 (NIV)*

We also see Paul in Romans 4 arguing from the Old Testament that God had intended to save the Gentiles all along. Paul also says in Acts 26:22-23:

> *[22] But God has helped me to this very day; so I stand here and testify to small and great alike. I am saying nothing beyond what the prophets and Moses said would happen— [23] that the Messiah would suffer and, as the first to rise from the dead, would bring the message of light to his own people and to the Gentiles." – Acts 26:22-23 (NIV)*

So in Ephesians, the writer isn't claiming that the salvation of the Gentiles is a totally new idea. Instead, the writer is claiming that it was a bit hazy what that meant until Jesus died and rose again. The second half of v5 makes it clear that **previous generations didn't have the clear revelation from the Holy Spirit that we now possess.**

GOING DEEPER

- What are some of the low points from your life? Looking back, can you see God at work in them or through them? Were you brought closer to Christ or pushed away from Christ through those low points?
- How can you see your small tasks from God in the broader view of God's amazing story? How does God want to be made known through your role of father, mother, sister, brother, child, or friend?
- What do you know clearly about God? What still seems fuzzy in your faith?

The First Ending Prayer (3:14-21)

This section is very similar to what Paul writes in Colossians 2:1-10. The basic point is that the writer is praying for the readers to be personally strengthened by the Holy Spirit dwelling in them. This indwelling of the Spirit affects the entire person from head to toe, from mind to soul. This culminates in a full knowledge of Christ's love, and this knowledge opens up every possibility for God to work in and through us. Let's go through these in turn.

Strengthened by the Holy Spirit. Verse 16 prays that God may "strengthen you with power through his Spirit in your inner being." It is quite possible that the hearers were somehow weakening or questioning their faith since the writer prays for their strengthening. It is interesting that the means of finding strength is by having the Spirit living within us. The idea of God living inside us was another new concept for Christianity. By way of comparison, here's what God told the Israelites about his presence:

> [8] "Then have them make a sanctuary for me, and I will dwell <u>among them</u>. [9] Make this tabernacle and all its furnishings exactly like the pattern I will show you. – Exodus 25:8-9 (NIV), emphasis added

Contrast God dwelling "among them" with what Jesus says:

> *On that day you will realize that I am in my Father, and you are in me, and <u>I am in you</u>. – John 14:20 (NIV), emphasis added*

The nearness of God is one of the hallmarks of the Christian faith, and it is one of its differentiators as well. It is easy to miss how important and life-changing this is. If God is just *near*, he might not be with me when I'm suffering. But if God is *in me*, he's right there through thick and thin. If God is just *near*, then when the door is shut and the Adversary (the "ruler of the kingdom of the air" from chapter two) is working against me, God may be outside the room. If God is *in me*, then the Adversary never has a clear shot at me when I'm alone. I have unfortunately known people who have committed suicide, people who have attempted suicide, and people who have thought about but ultimately rejected suicide. If God is just *near*, then he might have been absent from those battlegrounds. If God is *in us*, he was in the room battling on behalf of all those people. Don't underestimate the power and blessing of having God living within you. It's a big deal.

The Holy Spirit Transforms Our Whole Being. Verse 17 says that the point of having the Holy Spirit living within you is "so that Christ may dwell in your hearts through faith." At the time of this letter's writing, the "heart" encompassed a person's entire being [ARCH]. It included motivations, character, passions, interests, and everything else. This is almost a way of declaring by shorthand all of the statements Jesus makes in the Sermon on the Mount in Matthew 5-7. Jesus put everyone on notice that thoughts matter to God just as much as actions (Matthew 5:27-30). Jesus let us know that attitudes matter to God just as much as the end result (Matthew 5:21-26). Jesus told us that our character matters to God just as much as our intentions and results (Matthew 5:33-37). Jesus pointed out that our spiritual lives matter as much as our physical lives (Matthew 6). If we are citizens of the Kingdom of God, and if Christ lives within us through the Holy Spirit, then every part of our being belongs to the Kingdom. Our physical, spiritual, emotional, and mental selves are God's territory. Nothing is held back.

A Full Knowledge of Christ's Love, Resulting in God Working In and Thru Us. In verse 19 the writer prays that the church would "know this love that surpasses knowledge—that you may be filled to the measure of all the fullness of God." This verse is the key to unlocking the meaning of this section of chapter three. The Holy Spirit lives within us, allowing Christ to affect our whole being. But our knowledge of Christ's "love that surpasses knowledge" is what determines how much we are filled with the "fullness of God."

If we hold back part of our lives from God's presence and touch, it's because we haven't accepted Christ's love in that area. If we are worried about revealing our sins to God (who already knows them), it's because we haven't realized that Christ loves us even so. The knowledge of the love of Christ determines how much we allow God to fill and affect our lives.

In high school I had a conversation with a friend where I bemoaned God's approach to the universe. "If I were God," I told him, "and if I knew how everything would go down the tubes, I wouldn't have bothered to create any humans." Looking back, I made this statement because I believed God was really only interested in our behavior. Specifically, I thought God had an expansive list of things he wanted me to *not do*. Since I *did* many of the things on that list, and since everyone I knew and everyone I ever read about also *did* many of the things on that list, I reasoned that we were worthless. I missed the love of Christ that sees all of us as valuable, flaws and warts and behavior included. Missing the love of Christ limited how much I would allow God to work in me and through me.

GOING DEEPER

- Where do you need the strengthening of the Holy Spirit? Where is God battling on your behalf?
- How near or far does God feel to you right now? When have you felt closer to God? Further from him?
- Have you ever held back part of your life from the Holy Spirit's influence?
- Where do you doubt Christ's love for yourself or someone else? When have you stepped out in faith, confident that Christ loved you regardless of the outcome?

Ephesians 4

Devotional

As a pastor, I must confess that I find Paul's list of gifts (v11-12) to be rather troubling. After all, my two main roles (pastor and teacher) are the last two on the list! All you have to do to outrank me is to be an apostle, prophet, or evangelist. This seems totally unfair.

All kidding aside, these are some of my favorite passages in all of Scripture. In fact, piecing together Ephesians 4:7,12, and 15 gives you my purpose statement as a pastor:

"To each of us was given grace according to the measure of Christ's gift...to equip the saints for the work of ministry, for building up the body of Christ...[so] speaking the truth in love, we must grow up in every way into him who is the head, into Christ."

I believe it is my job to help other people discover their gift from God (v7) so they can use it to build up others (v12) in a way that lifts up the truth in a loving way (v15). When that happens it's a good day in ministry.

But I've noticed a problem. So many times people don't know their spiritual gifts. In fact, usually we take our gifts for granted. Do you always wind up leading things because no one else will? You might think everyone else can do it, but probably that's a gift for leadership. Do you always wind up organizing things? You might think everyone else can do it, but probably that's a gift of administration. Do you notice someone new or someone who is out of place and try to include them? You might think everyone else can do it, but probably that's a gift of hospitality. Do people come to you for advice? You might think everyone else could help them just as well, but probably that's a gift of wisdom.

We are generally terrible at identifying our own spiritual gifts because we think what comes naturally to us comes naturally to others. And then we all too often look at what comes naturally to someone else and wish it came naturally to us. Guess what? They're thinking the same thing about whatever comes naturally to you.

GOING DEEPER

- What do you do well but you think "everyone else can do it?"
- Think of some of the people who matter to you. Do you know some of their spiritual gifts or talents?
- Who can you ask to help you identify your spiritual gifts?
- Where has God used you in the past? Where might God want to use the gifts he gave you in the future?

The Church's Unity and Maturity (4:1-16)

Chapter four starts off with an appeal that is based off of the first three chapters of build-up. After the writer spent so much time detailing how God has broken down the barriers between us in Christ, he then pleads with the church to "keep the unity of the Spirit" (v3). The writer then states seven different ways we are "one" in v4-6. All three persons of the Trinity are stated, along with four ways that God works in our midst [REF]. Basically, the writer is saying, **"In Jesus, God broke down the barriers between us. Don't put them back up!"**

It is interesting to note, however, that the plea starts off by highlighting the *attitudes* that are necessary for unity to thrive in the church. Verse two highlights humility, gentleness, patience, and forbearance as evidence that the church community is interacting with each other from a place of love. This list of proper attitudes would not have been well received by the Greek culture of the day. This would have been a how-to manual for showing weakness [GLOB]. In fact, the only time such behavior would have been condoned is when a person of lower status showed proper deference to their superiors [IVP].

The writer is essentially encouraging the church to remember their dependence on God (humility), the value of the people around them in the church (gentleness), and humanity's ultimately flawed nature (patience) [WORD]. With these attitudes in mind, it is finally possible to have forbearance that springs from our mutual love for each other. *When* we disagree, if our tone is angry or arrogant or intolerant of differences then we are not living into our unity in love.

As a quick aside, we aren't 100% sure what Christ descending to the lower regions means in v9. It could mean earth, it could mean death, and it could refer to the Holy Spirit descending on Pentecost.

But the writer then pivots toward the differences within the church community. **While we have unity, we don't have uniformity. We are seeking unity in diversity**. In verses 7-13 we see that Christ has something special in mind for each individual person. Before we dig into the various roles in the church, let us first pause with thanksgiving for verses 7-8. Every single person has some gift, some measure of grace, that Christ wants to put into action on behalf of others. You are gifted!

While everyone is gifted, some have special roles in the church community. The "apostles" generally refers to the people who walked with Christ, though others (like Paul) received the title as they were sent out to start new churches [JNTC]. The apostolic role anchors all the others in the person and teachings of Christ. "Prophets" are tasked with speaking God's truth, "evangelists" share the Good News of Jesus Christ, and "pastors and teachers" help believers incorporate Christ in their minds and lives. But the real point is found in verses 12-13 – all the roles in the church are designed to promote healthy growth in the body of Christ (the Church). **The job of a church leader is to promote unity in diversity (v1-6), to help others use their gifts for others (v12), to grow in faith and knowledge of Jesus (v13), and to live Christ-like lives (v13).**

But what are spiritual gifts, and how do we use them for others? Paul writes elsewhere in Romans:

> *⁶ We have different gifts, according to the grace given to each of us. If your gift is prophesying, then prophesy in accordance with your faith; ⁷ if it is serving, then serve; if it is teaching, then teach; ⁸ if it is to encourage, then give encouragement; if it is giving, then give generously; if it is to lead, do it diligently; if it is to show mercy, do it cheerfully. – Romans 12:6-8 (NIV)*

To summarize, **a spiritual gift is something you do that brings you and other people closer to God without requiring much discipline from you**. The amount of conscious effort you expend to motivate yourself to action distinguishes between a gifting and a discipline.

For example, whenever I take a spiritual gift assessment, prayer always comes near the bottom of my gift list. That means I am consciously choosing to pray. I often start my church meetings and then retroactively offer a blessing because I forget that we're supposed to open the meeting with prayer. I have "prayer" as a checklist item in my personal devotional time because I would stop at reading and reflecting without that reminder. So while I do pray very regularly, it is always a choice and it is therefore a spiritual discipline instead of a spiritual gift.

By contrast, I do have the spiritual gift of leadership. I have to remind myself *not* to lead things. If we need to get from A to Z, I will naturally start organizing people, casting vision, and doing everything possible to get us there. I like to lead things. That's a spiritual gift instead of a spiritual discipline.

Does that mean I should focus on leadership and ignore prayer? Am I "off the hook" for praying simply because it's not my gift? Unfortunately, that's not how it works. Jesus frequently went off on his own to pray (Luke 5:16), and he assumed that we all would pray to our Father in heaven (Matthew 6:6). Even though it takes discipline, I'm still supposed to pray.

In a similar vein, if giving isn't your spiritual gift, that doesn't mean you don't have to give. Jesus also assumed that we would give to the poor, to the needy, and to the Temple (Matthew 6:2-3). If evangelism isn't your gift, that doesn't mean you get to blow off someone who God places on your path to share your story (Acts 1:8). All of the spiritual practices are expected of us, but some of them come naturally (spiritual gifts), and those are the ones God will tend to have you use most frequently. The others are still expected, but they take more discipline and effort.

Finally, verses 14-16 show that maturity is the result of adopting the attitudes required for unity and coming together to utilize our gifts (and disciplines) for others. The image for maturity is a full-grown adult [VINC]. As the writer talks about being tossed around and blown around I am reminded of my infant who is just trying to learn to crawl and walk. Sometimes he gets it all together and moves toward his goal. Other times he accidentally goes backwards (which is quite distressful apparently). When he gets too frustrated, he reverts to rolling toward his goal. There's no guarantee that his efforts will result in forward progress. In fact, sometimes when he's sitting and playing he just plops over for no apparent reason. That's the image of the infant in verse 14 – someone who is easily thrown off and often not making progress toward the goal.

The antidote to spiritual infanthood is to continue growing in both truth and love (v15). The evidence of spiritual adulthood is found in the humble spirit that promotes unity (v1-6), and using your spiritual gifts and disciplines to help others in Christ's name (v7-13).

GOING DEEPER

- Looking at the attitudes of unity that are encouraged in v1-6, which ones do you frequently exhibit and which ones do you frequently forget to exhibit?
- How do you react when there is diversity of opinion on important issues?
- What are your spiritual gifts? If you don't know, ask someone who knows you well. Spiritual gifts are often hard for us to see but easy for others to see.
- What spiritual practices require discipline for you?
- Who do you know who embodies the image of a mature spiritual adult from v14-16? Where could you grow in Christ's truth or Christ's love?

Living Into Our Spiritual Maturity (4:17-32)

Christianity always has this tension between the "already" and the "not yet." I like to think of this tension kind of like filming a prequel movie. The audience already knows where the story goes, but they don't know all the details for each character. For example, everyone knew Anakin Skywalker would become Darth Vader, but the exact progression wasn't known until we saw Star Wars Episodes I, II, and III. Fittingly, as with the Star Wars prequel trilogy, our own existence doesn't always live up to expectations!

For Christians, we know God's grand story. We know God wins. We know the climax of the story already happened when Jesus died and rose again. We know Jesus said he will come back again. We know there is a promise of resurrection at that time. But what does that mean for me, personally, on any random Tuesday? We know where the story is going, but we don't know how our own story will tie in.

This whole section serves to remind the readers that they are *already* new people in Christ (2 Corinthians 5:17), but they are *not yet* living into it fully. We are cast, as part of the prequel, to live into our destination identity more and more. We are supposed to show the character progression that is finalized in the ending of the main movie.

Verses 17-19 have a very different tone regarding Gentiles than the writer used in the first three chapters. I believe the point is to remind the readers that **they may be Gentiles by birth, but they should be Jewish in their definition of right and wrong** [IVP]. The first three chapters of Ephesians reminded the Gentile Christians that they are joined to the Covenant of Israel, and this section reminds them that their newfound citizenship extends to their daily lives.

The writer uses the image of clothing in verses 20-25 to illustrate an important point. This morning I looked in my closet, chose a particular pair of brown pants, a particular red shirt, and one of my two options for brown shoes. I had many options, but I picked this combination today. **If our attitudes and actions are like clothing, we always have a choice about which ones we put on and take off**. We all have natural inclinations away from God (Romans 3:23), but we always have a choice about how we act and behave (1 Corinthians 10:13). We are saved by grace, not good behavior (Ephesians 2:8-9), but we are "to be made new in the attitude of your minds; and to put on the new self, created to be like God in true righteousness and holiness" (Ephesians 4:23-24 NIV). There's that "already" and "not yet" thing again.

Specifically, verses 25-32 highlight five wardrobe choices for our daily lives [REF].

1. Put off lying (v25) and put on telling the truth (v25)
2. Put off rage (v26) and put on self-control (v27)
3. Put off stealing (v28) and put on useful work for others (v28)
4. Put off damaging words (v29) and put on helpful words (v29)
5. Put off emotions that condemn others (v31) and put on emotions that give life to others (v32)

First off, let me talk a little more about the negative emotions listed in v31 by looking at v26-27:

> [26] *"In your anger do not sin": Do not let the sun go down while you are still angry,* [27] *and do not give the devil a foothold.* – Ephesians 4:26-27 (NIV)

There is some debate about the meaning of the Greek words in verse 26. It might mean "be angry but don't sin" or it might mean "even when you're angry don't sin." It's unclear whether the writer is condoning the emotion of anger but redirecting it or implying that anger is regrettable but ultimately unavoidable. Either way, anger that is stored up overnight allows the Adversary room to maneuver in your heart (v27). Compare these verses with Psalm 4 and Hosea 7:

> [4]*Tremble and do not sin; when you are on your beds, search your hearts and be silent.* [5]*Offer the sacrifices of the righteous and trust in the Lord.* – Psalm 4:4-5 (NIV)

> [6]*Their hearts are like an oven; they approach him with intrigue. Their passion smolders all night; in the morning it blazes like a flaming fire.* – Hosea 7:6 (NIV)

Taken together, Ephesians 4, Psalm 4, and Hosea 7 imply that we can choose to direct our anger in a God-honoring direction or a God-dishonoring direction. The choice, like what clothes we wear, is ours to make. I generally break anger down into two broad categories: anger at a person and anger at a situation. A God-honoring direction for anger at a situation is best typified by Jesus driving out those who were unjustly charging for sacrifices at the Temple (John 2:13-17). He used his anger to make the world a better place.

Anger at a person requires a different approach. Jesus says in Matthew 18:15-17 that we are to talk directly with people when we are angry, and in Matthew 5:23-24 he says that reconciliation with another person is more important than offering gifts at the altar. When I talk with couples before their weddings, I always tell them that bitterness is a canary in the mineshaft for their future marriage. Whenever they notice bitterness toward their spouse creeping into their thoughts, they must immediately seek help to talk through the issues. Otherwise, as v27 says, the Adversary will go to work in their hearts.

I also believe it is important to note that **our words can "grieve the Holy Spirit"** (v29-30). First of all, notice that the Holy Spirit can grieve. I see this as an affirmation that the Holy Spirit is a person, not an idea or a thing. Not only is the Holy Spirit a person, but the Spirit cares deeply about our words, their intent, and their result. I don't know about you, but I often find that the path between the emotions in v31 and my words is rather short sometimes.

GOING DEEPER

- Looking at the five wardrobe choices from v25-32, which one might God be calling you to "put off?" Which one might you "put on?"
- When have you processed anger in a God-honoring way? When have you processed anger in a God-dishonoring way?
- How do you relate to the Holy Spirit? Does the Spirit seem to be a person or a thing to you?

Ephesians 5

Devotional

I have always loved comic books and graphic novels. One comic book introduced Bizarro World – a universe where everything is the opposite of our expectations. Bat Man carries, not a utility belt, but a *futility* belt in Bizarro World.

Whenever I hear someone quote Ephesians 5:22 on its own, "Wives submit to your own husbands, as to the Lord," I think of Bizarro World. That verse quoted alone has been used to justify abuse. That verse quoted on its own has been used to "put women in their place" and absolve men of any responsibility. That verse quoted on its own makes total sense…in Bizarro World.

First off, when you look in the Greek the word for "submit" is…not there. There isn't a verb in that sentence. It just says, "Wives to your husbands as to the Lord." The verb is inferred from the previous verse. Ephesians 5:21 says, "submitting to one another out of reverence for Christ." So that's the real context. Paul is saying that husbands and wives and indeed everyone else should submit to each other in the name of Christ who came to serve, not to be served (Mark 10:45).

So wives, you can honor the servant Christ by showing that servant attitude toward your husband. And husbands, you're not off the hook! In fact, if you keep reading Paul gives husbands more than double the instruction of wives starting in v25. No wife will be surprised that husbands have to be told multiple times to get the point :-) He tells husbands you can honor the servant Christ by sacrificing for your wife just as Christ sacrificed his life for you.

And in case we missed the point, Paul even summarizes it for us in v33: "Each of you, however, should love his wife as himself, and a wife should respect her husband." Why don't we quote that verse instead of going all Bizarro World and just quoting the part about the wives?

In short, Paul says that we should all adopt a servant mindset toward each other, just as Christ served us. To illustrate it, he paints the picture of a Christ-like marriage where both husband and wife serve each other 100%, where the wife knows she's loved and the husband knows he's respected.

But here's the problem now that we understand what Paul means – now we have to put it into practice in our own relationships.

GOING DEEPER

- When has someone surprised you by showing you a servant heart?
- When have you been able to have a servant heart toward another person?
- On a scale of 1-10, how much are you showing Christ's servant heart in your own relationships (friends, spouses, family, etc)?
- If you are married, how can you demonstrate to your spouse both love and respect?

From Darkness to Light (5:1-20)

The first two verses of this chapter are some of the most challenging. **We are to pattern our lives on God, especially as seen in Jesus' sacrifice on our behalf** (v2). Chrysostom, one of the influential early Christian teachers, wrote about these verses:

> *You spare your friends. He spared his enemies. ... He suffered on his enemies' behalf. This is the fragrant offering, the acceptable sacrifice. If you suffer for your enemies as a fragrant offering, you too become an acceptable sacrifice, even if you die. This is what it means to imitate God.* [ACC]

This reminds me of when I was younger. I loved to walk the aisles of bookstores, perusing the titles even in sections that generally held no interest for me. I remember spotting some books that touted Jesus as the perfect CEO or business leader. But even back then it seemed strange to me. After all, if a CEO told investors that the company would be sacrificing itself for others, I doubt the stock price would go up. But that's the pattern we are given for our lives – a willingness to place others, even enemies and rivals, ahead of our own wellbeing. I don't know about you, but I still have a considerable distance to grow in this aspect of my faith. I find it difficult but certainly possible to pray for my enemies and want the best for them (Matthew 5:44), but being willing to suffer on their behalf is a whole different level.

The writer then shifts back to the ways that our growing spiritual maturity (from chapter four) should manifest itself in our lives. **Verses 3-7 add sexuality and popularity to the list of wardrobe changes that allow us to show maturity or immaturity in our faith.** The word for "sexual immorality" is a general term that is used throughout the Bible to refer to pretty much every kind of sexual sin [VINE]. The word for "impurity" is used to connote a lack of health physically and morally, generally arising from bad teachings about what is healthy [VINE]. Taken together in the context of this letter, I believe the writer is telling the readers to take their cues about healthy sexuality from Scripture rather than culture. Every generation battles the various forces vying to define the truth about our sexuality, and here the writer encourages each generation to approach the battle using Scripture, not just our own instincts and what our culture tells us.

Verse five seems unfairly hash, so we should give it a little more attention. It says:

> *For of this you can be sure: No immoral, impure or greedy person—such a person is an idolater—has any inheritance in the kingdom of Christ and of God.*
> *– Ephesians 5:5 (NIV)*

First off, an "idolater" is someone who looks to something else for ultimate truth and meaning rather than God [VINE]. So a person who defines sexual health without asking God or a "greedy" person who defines their needs and wants without asking God is worshiping something other than God. But does that person lose their place in heaven because of this? Well "inheritance" in the New Testament usually doesn't refer to our salvation, it refers to the gift of transformation in our lives *today* as a result of our salvation in Jesus [VINE]. In other words, this verse implies that a person who defines sexual health and needs and wants without asking God – an idolater – is missing out on a better life that is found in being guided by Christ. **Our "inheritance" in the kingdom is the gift of a better life when we follow God's directions.** This better life isn't free from struggle (James 1:2), but it is better nonetheless.

When we look at verses four and six, we see the writer's admonishment to not be caught up in the rat race of popularity contests. We are first told to avoid "obscenity, foolish talk or coarse joking." These words remind me of when I was in the audience for a standup comedy contest. Some of the comedians were very smooth and knew how to use pacing and audience expectations to their advantage to make a point or at least make people laugh. Others, however, wielded their jokes with all the finesse of an elephant using chopsticks. Unable to produce the desired result, they thought that a few more expletives would make it funnier. They were seeking cheap laughs by any means, and that's the image used in these verses. **If we are willing to say and do anything to receive the momentary approval of other people, we are chasing after the god of popularity.**

Verses 8-20 draw a contrast between living in darkness and living in light (v8), between foolishness (v17) and wisdom (v15). I believe the main point can be seen in verse 18:

> *Do not get drunk on wine, which leads to debauchery. Instead, be filled with the Spirit – Ephesians 5:18 (NIV)*

The phrase "drunk on wine" doesn't refer to an occasional drink. It implies a prolonged and repetitive state of inebriation. It's a habitual escape from life through chemicals in general and alcohol in particular. Instead of trying to escape life, however, the writer instead encourages us to be "filled with the Spirit." So **living in darkness is when we try to escape our troubles. Living in the light, by contrast, means entering life's struggles with the Holy Spirit (v18) and the Christian community (v19-20) walking alongside you.**

GOING DEEPER

- How hard or easy is it for you to pray for your enemies, want the best for them, and even sacrifice on their behalf? Have you ever seen someone do this?
- How do you define sexual health? How do you define a healthy level for your needs and wants? What Scriptures influence those definitions? What have you heard from God in prayer?
- Many people see Christianity as a list of "don'ts." What's on the "don't" list as a result of your faith, and what's on the "do" list as a result of your faith?

- When life is a struggle, do you try to escape? How might the Spirit and the Christian community walk alongside you instead?

The Christian Family (5:21-33)

There are several places in the Bible that address the family or the household. Collectively, these are known as the "household codes." These codes address the relationships between husbands and wives, parents and children, and masters and slaves. Given the content, it is unsurprising that these sections of Scripture have some of the most painful histories of use and misuse. The main household codes are attributed to Paul (Colossians 3:18-4:1, Titus 2:1-10, Ephesians 5:21-6:9) and Peter (1 Peter 2:18-3:7).

I think it's first important to note a major assumption made by Paul and Peter. The early church remembered Jesus saying things such as:

> *And he said to them, "Truly I tell you, some who are standing here will not taste death before they see that the kingdom of God has come with power." – Mark 9:1 (NIV)*

As a result, they assumed that Jesus' return would be very, very soon. As the years stretched on and the original followers of Jesus started to reach the end of their lives, Paul even had to address the issue.

> *13 Brothers and sisters, we do not want you to be uninformed about those who sleep in death, so that you do not grieve like the rest of mankind, who have no hope. 14 For we believe that Jesus died and rose again, and so we believe that God will bring with Jesus those who have fallen asleep in him. 15 According to the Lord's word, we tell you that we who are still alive, who are left until the coming of the Lord, will certainly not precede those who have fallen asleep. 16 For the Lord himself will come down from heaven, with a loud command, with the voice of the archangel and with the trumpet call of God, and the dead in Christ will rise first. 17 After that, we who are still alive and are left will be caught up together with them in the clouds to meet the Lord*

in the air. And so we will be with the Lord forever. ¹⁸ Therefore encourage one another with these words. – 1 Thessalonians 4:13-18 (NIV)

Some of the admonishments in these and other Bible passages should be seen within the context of the assumed imminent return of Christ to remake and redeem all things. As we will see in the next chapter of Ephesians, Paul did not view the present order of the world as a happy arrangement. But if Jesus was coming any day to take care of it, why should they get in his way? It was only later, once Christians realized that it would be a while before Jesus came again, that a social transformation movement really developed. In fact, when Martin Luther King, Jr. was accused of being an extremist, "Dr. King said that he stood in a long line of extremists, including the prophet Amos, Jesus, the apostle Paul, the Protestant reformer Martin Luther, Thomas Jefferson and Abraham Lincoln" (emphasis added) [WEB6].

Paul's encouragement to slaves, for example, to just hang in there until Jesus comes again should be seen in this context. Obviously Dr. King and others in the civil rights movement pulled from different quotes from Paul, and they were able to do so because Paul condemns many of the social wrongs that still plague us today. **Paul's diagnosis of the problems in society were spot on, his prescribed solution (Jesus) was spot on, but his recommendation for human action on social justice (just wait) was based on an incorrect assumption about the timing of Jesus' return.**

Now we can move to the text in front of us, which is targeted at husbands and wives. In some Bibles you will see a heading inserted between verses 21 and 22, but I find that difficult to justify. To see why, here are the two verses in question:

> *²¹ Submit to one another out of reverence for Christ. ²² Wives, submit yourselves to your own husbands as you do to the Lord. – Ephesians 5:22-23 (NIV)*

When you look in the Greek, you'll notice that the word "submit" isn't present in verse 22. It is assumed and carried over from verse 21. If the two verses are so correlated that they share a verb, it seems strange to split them apart. The word "submit" is usually a military term that connotes getting into proper formation [VINE]. With that image, when we "submit to one another" we have each other's backs and we are aligned in the same direction (which is Christ). When wives are encouraged to "submit yourselves to your own husbands as you do to the Lord" it's the same. Have your husband's back and align in the same direction (which is Christ). Since this is a military term, another way to see this is, "**Wives, go to battle for Christ *with* your husband, not *against* your husband.**"

The next few verses, which talk about the husband as the "head" of the wife, contain another military image. The first ships to land on D-Day were the "head" of the invasion of Europe in World War II. They were exposed to the fiercest opposition, and they secured a safer landing zone for the troops who followed. Similarly, Christ was the "head" of our redemption. He took initiative on the cross and didn't wait for us to make the first move. He entered the battle on our behalf, before we even knew there was a battle to be won. As with Christ and the church, as with the first ships on D-Day, the husband is to take initiative, enter the hardest part of the battle, and be a Christ-honoring husband before worrying about whether his wife is being a Christ-honoring wife [JNTC]. As with Christ being the "head" of the church on the cross, the husband's role of "head" is a duty to serve rather than a demand to be obeyed.

It is also curious to me that we don't hear more quotes about the obligations of husbands from verses 25-33. Husbands are given more than twice the amount of instructions as wives, but we don't hear these verses thrown about. The key for husbands is in verse 25:

> *²⁵ Husbands, love your wives, just as Christ loved the church and gave himself up for her. – Ephesians 5:25 (NIV)*

Once again the standard for husbands is Christ's self-sacrifice on the cross. Continuing the D-Day analogy, husbands are here told to be willing to take a bullet for their wives. If you've ever heard verse 22 used to justify abuse or imbalanced power structures, I bet you didn't hear verse 25 at the same time. In fact, I bet they skipped the rest of this chapter altogether, because it lines out an incredibly challenging standard for husbands to live up to. **I would summarize the duties of husbands as follows**:

1. Take the initiative in being Christ-like in your marriage (v23)
2. Be willing to take a bullet for your wife (v25)
3. Let your wife know you love her (v28)
4. Work on your marriage as often as you eat (v29)
5. Keep working on your marriage until you and your wife are "one" (v31)

That could take a lifetime! **The shorthand version, for both husbands and wives, is found in verse 33**:

> *However, each one of you also must love his wife as he loves himself, and the wife must respect her husband. – Ephesians 5:33 (NIV)*

GOING DEEPER

- Given that we are to be ready for Christ's return at any moment (Matthew 24:44), but it has also been almost 2000 years, how do you live your life in light of our ultimate hope of Christ's return?
- Where might God be encouraging you to take initiative and be loving first?
- When have you been in a relationship that was working well at the time? What made it work well?
- When have you been in a relationship that wasn't working well at the time? What made it struggle?
- If you have a spouse, how can you tangibly show love or respect this week?

Ephesians 6

Devotional

If you've ever watched *Lord of the Rings*, you know the scene where Gandalf the wizard faces off against a dragon-like creature called a Balrog. Once the rest of the group has safely crossed the bridge, Gandalf turns toward the creature and declares, "I am a servant of the Secret Fire, wielder of the Flame of Anor. You CANNOT PASS!" A battle ensues until Gandalf tricks the Balrog by destroying the bridge as it crosses. He turns, relieved that the battle is over, until the Balrog manages to catch his foot with a whip, dragging the wizard down into the abyss with it.

We are able to fight against evil when it has a face. We are able to muster our courage and brazenly declare who we are and what we stand for when the battle is upon us. But when we turn around, relieved at our victory, that's often when we fall.

Paul writes in v11 that we need "the whole armor of God, so that you may be able to stand against the wiles of the devil." We need the "belt of truth", the "breastplate of righteousness," the ability "to proclaim the gospel of peace," the "shield of faith," the "helmet of salvation," and "the sword of the Spirit, which is the word of God" (v14-17).

We need to know God's truth, or when we're not on guard the adversary will trick us with falsehood. We need to seek righteousness in our lives, or the adversary will trick us into justifying whatever we're doing. We need a reservoir of faith, or the adversary will slowly drain us with worry and doubt. We need to know God's Word, or the adversary will trick us just as Adam and Eve were tricked when the serpent asked, "Did God really say…" (Genesis 3:1).

Sometimes the most difficult battles in our lives are the ones we think are already over. Just ask Gandalf.

GOING DEEPER

- What are some struggles in your life that you have overcome?
- How might your past struggles rear their ugly heads again?
- How do you build up your spirit with the various pieces of the armor of God? For example, how do you grow in

knowing God's truth or seeking righteousness or accepting your salvation?
- What battle are you facing now, and how can your faith community provide reinforcements?

Serve Christ, Not People (6:1-9)

There are two main points in this section. The first point is seen in verse 7.

Serve wholeheartedly, as if you were serving the Lord, not people – Ephesians 6:7 (NIV)

As we saw in Ephesians 5:21, the pattern for Christian households is mutual submission (getting in formation together) as a result of our faith in Christ. Ephesians 6:7 takes that one step further, implying that Christians are to act in a Christ-like way regardless of their circumstances. The writer of Ephesians doesn't put any conditions on this. For children, be Christ-like toward your parents even if they aren't Christ-like toward you. For fathers, be Christ-like toward your children even if they aren't Christ-like toward you. For slaves, be Christ-like toward your masters even if they aren't Christ-like toward you. For masters, be Christ-like toward your slaves even if they aren't Christ-like toward you. Regardless of our circumstances, we have the ability to choose (or "put on" from Ephesians 4) a Christ-like response.

In my time as a pastor, I have walked with several people through dark times in their marriages and their family relationships. It is very common to hear a plethora of reasons why a person is behaving in a certain way. Maybe one person is lashing out in anger because the other party is "always" insulting them. Or maybe someone has given up because "nothing ever changes." The writer of Ephesians would probably reply that those are nice explanations, but they aren't good excuses. **The mandate to be Christ-like toward other people is not predicated on their Christ-like behavior toward us**.

The second point is found at the end of verse 9.

you know that he who is both their Master and yours is in heaven, and there is no favoritism with him. – Ephesians 6:9 (NIV)

As I mentioned before, Paul probably focused too much on not upsetting the social applecart since Jesus would be coming to clean everything up very soon. But he also laid the conceptual foundation for later social justice movements. With regard to slavery, Paul did not advocate for a worldwide abolition of slavery. But he undermined the justification for slavery in Ephesians 6:9 and asked for the release of a newly-converted slave named Onesimus in the letter to Philemon. Early Christian slaveowners in America were actually hesitant to share the Gospel with their slaves, because they were afraid they would have to free them once they converted based on Paul's letter to Philemon [IVP].

In the book of Ephesians, we have seen that God sees Jews and Gentiles the same (Ephesians 2), God sees husbands and wives the same (Ephesians 5), God sees children and parents the same (Ephesians 6), and God sees slaves and masters the same (Ephesians 6:9). **God does not see a difference between race, gender, age, or economic status. In other words, we all have the same standing with God. No one can claim pride of place based on birth or wealth.**

Contrast that sweeping statement with the publications in the 1800's that argued that African Americans were biologically inferior to whites [WEB7]. They must have ignored Ephesians to make that argument.

Even though slavery in the Roman Empire was based on economics, not race [ARCH], early Christian leaders were squarely against it. Here's what John Chrysostom, the Bishop of Constantinople in the late fourth century, wrote about slavery:

> *God's law does not recognize these social distinctions. If anyone should ask where slavery comes from and why it has stolen into human life—for I know that many are keen to ask such things and desire to learn—I shall tell you. It is avarice that brought about slavery. It is acquisitiveness, which is insatiable. This is not the original human condition. Remember that Noah had no slave, nor Abel nor Seth nor those after them. This horrid thing was begotten by sin.* [ACC]

So how did we get from Paul claiming all are equal in God's eyes and early Christian leaders calling slavery a terrible sin to Christian leaders using Scripture to argue in favor of race-specific slavery in America in the 1800's? One word: power.

Christianity had an on-again-off-again relationship with the authorities in Rome until the late 300's. After that, Christianity and the Roman Empire were increasingly intertwined. After the collapse of the Roman Empire, the church remained in control of many of the levers of power in Europe during the Middle Ages. And so, as the Church began to acquire wealth on its own, as it began to have something to lose, it began to see slavery in a different light. For instance, in 595 Pope Gregory sent a priest on a mission to purchase some Pagan slaves to work the church lands [WEB8]. Later on, as the kings of Spain and Portugal were attempting to beat back Muslim invaders from Northern Africa, they were given permission to enslave Muslims [WEB8]. In the United States, slavery was justified as a means of converting slaves to Christianity [WEB7]. In all three of these instances, when the Church was intertwined with the vested interests of those in power, faith was bent to the will of the powerful.

This is a strong warning against the urge to pick and choose which Scriptures we believe. Almost any agenda can be endorsed with the proper application of blinders while reading the Bible.

GOING DEEPER

- As you consider being Christ-like toward others, who in your life has made that easy for you? Who has made it difficult?
- When has someone shown you Christ-like grace that you didn't deserve?
- Have you ever thought someone else didn't have value? Has anyone ever treated you as if you had no value?
- What parts of the Bible do you struggle with or wish weren't there?
- When has a part of the Bible challenged or changed what you were doing?

The Daily Battle (6:10-24)

Many times throughout Ephesians, the writer has used military terms and imagery. The letter closes with a description of the battle all followers of Christ must fight daily. Verse 12 reminds the reader that **our daily battle isn't against a foe on the earthly plane, but against the "ruler of the kingdom of the air" from Ephesians 2. This is a battle we cannot win on our own, but with the Lord's "mighty power" we are able to "stand [our] ground."**

I find it interesting that all but one of the images used in this chapter are defensive rather than offensive. For instance, the writer talks about "standing" three times, but never once mentions advancing forward. This reminds me of Philippians 4:

> *I know what it is to be in need, and I know what it is to have plenty. I have learned the secret of being content in any and every situation, whether well fed or hungry, whether living in plenty or in want. I can do all this through him who gives me strength.* – *Philippians 4:12-13 (NIV)*

While verse 13 is often quoted and even written by athletes on their hats or jerseys, the context is about having peace and surviving whether you're winning or losing at the moment. It's like saying, "I'll be OK even if we lose today." That's probably not going to make it on an inspirational poster any time soon!

But that's the image of "standing firm" or "standing your ground" from Ephesians 6. We aren't assured that we will avoid the battle, we are assured that through Christ we can survive the battle. **We aren't given tips on how to dodge the Adversary's attacks, we are given tips on how to let God take the force like a soldier's armor.**

I am a big Star Wars fan, and the repeated use of the phrase "full armor" brings to mind the difference between Stormtroopers and Jedi. The Jedi always seem to be wearing robes. Cotton isn't known for being an effective piece of armor. Stormtroopers, however, wear a gleaming white full body suit of clamshell armor. This armor protects them against every attack…unless it's coming from the heroes, of course. A Jedi wears robes because they are experts at dodging attacks, and a Stormtrooper wears armor because they can't dodge the attacks. The writer of Ephesians would say that our dodging abilities are more like Stormtroopers than Jedi. The Adversary's attacks are going to hit us again and again, so we need the "full armor of God."

The full equipment list is as follows:
1. God's truth (v14)
2. Righteousness, which is right behavior toward God and others (v14)
3. Christ's peace (v15)
4. Faith despite the Adversary flinging lies at you (v16)
5. Assurance of your salvation (or deliverance) by Christ (v17)
6. Knowledge of the Word of God and understanding that is given by the Spirit (v17)

One last observation requires backing up to verse 11.

> *Put on the full armor of God, so that you can take your stand against the devil's schemes. – Ephesians 6:11 (NIV)*

Imagine a battle that is being waged across a wide field. As the infantry duke it out in the middle, the enemy commander sends his cavalry around the back and now one side is surrounded. The enemy commander used a "scheme" (v11) to probably win the battle. Unlike a normal set of armor, which can't protect the soldier from the wily enemy commander, the "full armor of God" can protect us against the schemes of the Adversary.

For example, I knew a man who liked to joke that his greatest temptation was french fries. Many years later we discovered he had an affair. Apparently french fries weren't his greatest temptation after all. He was deceived about his weaknesses, but the Adversary knew where to attack. He needed the "belt of truth" to protect against that scheme.

The writer ends with an appeal to pray "on all occasions," with "all kinds of prayers," for "all the Lord's people" (v18). I believe there is a connection between the one offensive weapon mentioned ("the sword of the Spirit") and this encouragement to pray. We may only be able to stand firm rather than advance in our daily battle, but through the Word of God and prayer God can cause us to move forward rather than stand still.

GOING DEEPER

- What do you struggle with in your everyday life?
- How has God saved you from the attacks of the Adversary in the past?
- Looking at the list of equipment from v14-17, which ones are in good shape and which ones need a blacksmith to repair or build up?
- Where could you use prayer? Where could others use prayer? Where could our world use prayer?

Summary and Major Take-Aways

Now that you have read the whole book of Ephesians, how have you been transformed? If we spend time growing in knowledge of the Bible but never apply it to our lives, we are stopping too soon. My favorite baseball player when I was growing up was Rickey Henderson, and he played for the Oakland A's. There is a story (which Rickey recently confirmed) [WEB9] that he received a million dollar check from the A's. Since he had dreamed of being a millionaire one day when he was a kid, he framed the check and placed it on his wall. A while later the team's accountants discovered that Rickey had never cashed the check. They called him up and found out it was still on his wall! If we grow in knowledge but never change as a result of what we have learned, we are leaving God's check of new life uncashed on our walls. Cash the check, accept God's gift, and live a new life. After all, "knowledge puffs up while love builds up" (1 Corinthians 8:1b NIV).

As a reminder, here are the major sections for each chapter:
- Reminder and Encouragement (1:3-14)
- Thanksgiving and Prayer (1:15-23)
- Amazing Grace (2:1-10)
- Breaking Down the Wall of Division (2:11-22)
- The Mystery Revealed (3:1-13)
- The First Ending Prayer (3:14-21)
- The Church's Unity and Maturity (4:1-16)
- Living Into Our Spiritual Maturity (4:17-32)
- From Darkness to Light (5:1-20)
- The Christian Family (5:21-33)
- Serve Christ, Not People (6:1-9)
- The Daily Battle (6:10-24)

GOING DEEPER

- What did you learn for the first time? Were you reminded of anything that you had let fade into the background?
- How has God challenged you in some way through the book of Ephesians?
- How as God affirmed you in some way through the book of Ephesians?
- Where might Christ want to do something in your heart or life as a result of this study?

Background

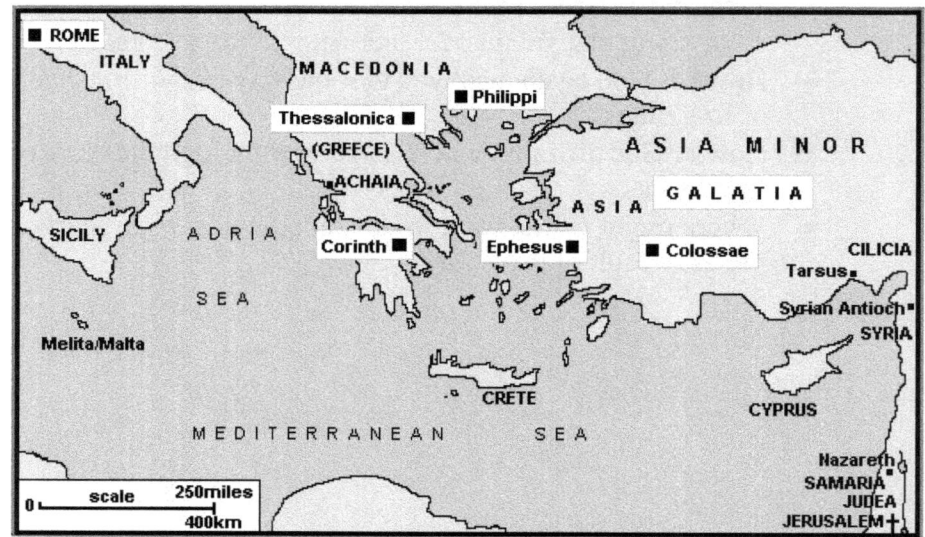

Figure 2. Map by Gordon Smith

Ephesus the City

Ephesus was located on the Western coast of present-day Turkey (see map), which was known as Asia Minor. In Roman times it was known as "the first and greatest metropolis of Asia" [EAS]. While archaeologists aren't certain of the population at the time, some estimates go as high as 225,000 [ERD].

Ephesus was also a major trade city. In addition to an accessible port that helped connect Europe and Asia, the city brought together two major trade routes that provided access to the rest of Asia Minor [ISBE]. As the starting point for any journey through Asia Minor, the Book of Revelation was sent to Ephesus first (Rev. 2-3) and from there made the rounds to the other churches.

Major trade cities had everything available to them. They had the best and the worst that civilization had to offer. On the plus side, Ephesus was home to the well-equipped Library of Celsus and an Amphitheatre that could hold more than 25,000 people (see pictures). On the seedier side, archaeologists have found markers carved in the stone sidewalk to clearly guide sailors from the port to a house of prostitution [ISBE].

Figure 3. Amphitheatre photo by Norman Herr

Figure 4. Library of Celsus photo by Svetlana Tikhonova

Figure 5. Temple of Artemis engraving by Martin Heemskerck

Easily the most important structure in Ephesus was the Temple of Artemis, one of the Seven Wonders of the Ancient World (see painting). Most of the cultures around the Mediterranean and Middle East had some version of Artemis worshipped under a different name. Artemis was portrayed as a kind of Mother Earth personified, with images of nursing, birth, and new life surrounding her. It is possible that the statue of Artemis inside the Temple was at least partially constructed from a meteorite (Acts 20:3).

As the Temple *par excellence* for Artemis worship, Ephesus had a significant portion of its economy derived from tourism, pilgrimages, and the sale of images of Artemis. Paul ran into this economic reality in Acts 19:23ff as the church in Ephesus reached a large enough size to threaten the craftsmen whose livelihoods were dependent on Artemis:

> *About that time there arose a great disturbance about the Way. [24] A silversmith named Demetrius, who made silver shrines of Artemis, brought in a lot of business for the craftsmen there. [25] He called them together, along with the workers in related trades, and said: "You know, my friends, that we receive a good income from this business. [26] And you see and hear how this fellow Paul has convinced and led*

> *astray large numbers of people here in Ephesus and in practically the whole province of Asia. He says that gods made by human hands are no gods at all.[27] There is danger not only that our trade will lose its good name, but also that the temple of the great goddess Artemis will be discredited; and the goddess herself, who is worshiped throughout the province of Asia and the world, will be robbed of her divine majesty." – Acts 19:23-27 (NIV)*

In many ways, Ephesus was a keystone. The residents of the city had access to ideas and goods from around the known world. They were passionate in their worship of Artemis. They were at the intersection of so many trade routes that you could reach almost anywhere from the port or the roads. If the church took root in Ephesus, it would have the opportunity to spread far and wide. But Ephesus was far more challenging than other cities for all the same reasons. For a modern analogy, think of Ephesus as Broadway. You have to be the cream of the crop to be an actor or singer on Broadway. If Christianity (or the Way as it was known at that time) could make it in Ephesus (Broadway), it could make it elsewhere.

Ephesus the Church

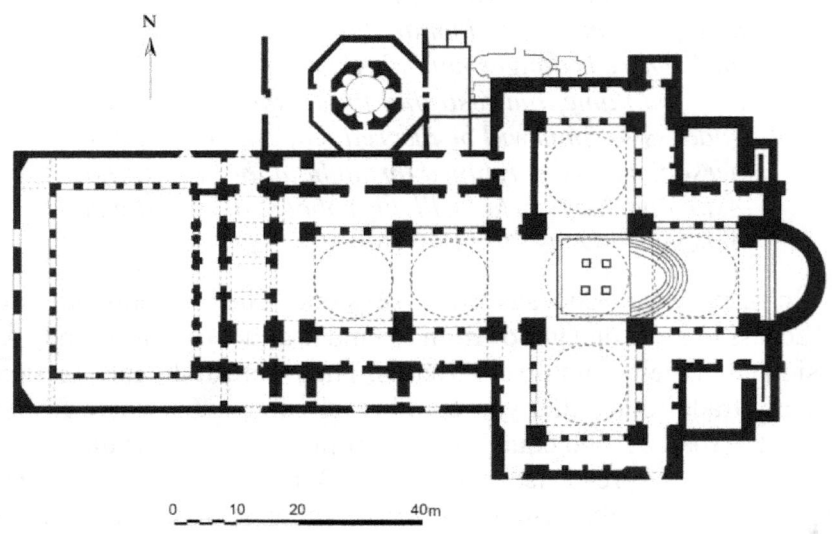

Figure 6. Floorplan of Basilica of St. John by Marsyas

The church in Ephesus played a major role in early Christianity. Some of the most influential early leaders were part of the church. Paul planted the church (Acts 18-19), Apollos was trained at Ephesus (Acts 18:24-28), Aquila and Priscilla were left to help grow the church (Acts 18:19-20), Timothy is widely thought to have been the first bishop of Ephesus (1 Timothy 1:3), and it is possible that Onesimus, the slave Paul asks Philemon to free for ministry, was the same Onesimus mentioned by Ignatius of Antioch in a letter as the second bishop of Ephesus. Finally, Ephesus is the traditional ministry location of the Apostle John. It is thought that John wrote his Gospel from Ephesus and was eventually buried in the city as well [ERD].

The church in Ephesus was also the first church mentioned in the Book of Revelation:

> [1] *"To the angel of the church in Ephesus write: These are the words of him who holds the seven stars in his right hand and walks among the seven golden lampstands.* [2] *I know your deeds, your hard work and your perseverance. I know that you cannot tolerate wicked people, that you have tested those who claim*

> *to be apostles but are not, and have found them false. ³ You have persevered and have endured hardships for my name, and have not grown weary. ⁴ Yet I hold this against you: You have forsaken the love you had at first. ⁵ Consider how far you have fallen! Repent and do the things you did at first. If you do not repent, I will come to you and remove your lampstand from its place. ⁶ But you have this in your favor: You hate the practices of the Nicolaitans, which I also hate. ⁷ Whoever has ears, let them hear what the Spirit says to the churches. To the one who is victorious, I will give the right to eat from the tree of life, which is in the paradise of God.*
> *– Revelation 2:1-7 (NIV)*

This important city filled with important leaders was also apparently deemed important by God. The early church saw many miracles, but even they were astounded by what happened in Ephesus as Paul was planting the church:

> *¹¹ God did extraordinary miracles through Paul, ¹² so that even handkerchiefs and aprons that had touched him were taken to the sick, and their illnesses were cured and the evil spirits left them. – Acts 19:11-12 (NIV)*

The church in Ephesus played a major part in Paul's life. In addition to the three months he spent planting the church, he later returned for three years – far longer than most of his stops. He also made sure to see the leaders of the church before his final fateful journey to Jerusalem that resulted in his arrest (Acts 20:13-38).

Context for the Letter

Most of Paul's letters contain a rather obvious reason for writing the letter. For instance, Paul indicates in 1 Corinthians that he's writing in response to a request for his advice (1 Corinthians 7:1) and that he is aware of major divisions within the church (1 Corinthians 1:10). But the letter to the Ephesians doesn't have a clear-cut motivation. It is possible that this letter was written simply to encourage the church. It is also possible that this letter was addressed to multiple churches (more on this below), so it's less specific than some of Paul's other letters.

There is actually considerable debate over the recipients of the letter. Archaeologists have uncovered many letters, papyri, scrolls, and the like that contain portions of what we now know as the New Testament. These various texts are basically the same 95% of the time, and most of the remaining differences are very minor (switching "Jesus Christ" for "Christ Jesus" for example). Sometimes, however, there are meaningful differences. When this occurs, translators must choose some means of prioritizing the texts and deciding which one is "most original." One of the common ways that modern scholars pick one set of texts over another is by determining the date of original authorship. So, for example, if one text was written in the year 110 AD and another was written in 745 AD, modern scholars tend to give the oldest text the benefit of the doubt for being the most original.

The letter to the Ephesians starts off this way in the NIV: "Paul, an apostle of Christ Jesus by the will of God, To God's holy people in Ephesus, the faithful in Christ Jesus" (Ephesians 1:1). But many of those oldest texts don't have the phrase "in Ephesus." They just address the letter "To God's holy people, faithful in Christ Jesus." There isn't a location named. To solve this riddle, some scholars propose that this was written as a cyclical letter that started in Ephesus and then was passed around to the other churches in Asia Minor [DBI].

Another riddle comes from the author. If this is truly a letter from Paul, it is puzzling that there are so many subtle differences between how it is written and how the other letters from Paul are written [ISBE]. Greek words that Paul uses frequently in other letters are avoided or used very differently in this letter. The author writes that he has only "heard" of their faith (Ephesians 1:15), but Paul spent more than three years with them. When the author writes in Ephesians 2:20 that the church is "built on the foundation of the apostles and prophets, with Christ Jesus himself as the chief cornerstone" (NIV), it directly contradicts what Paul writes in 1 Corinthians 3:11, "For no one can lay any foundation other than the one already laid, which is Jesus Christ" (NIV). Furthermore, two major themes from the letters that are definitely written by Paul are the ongoing development of Jewish and Gentile Christianity and the imminent return of Jesus Christ. In Ephesians, however, Christianity is addressed as a predominantly Gentile church and the return of Jesus is now acknowledged as possibly happening over many generations (Ephesians 3:21). You can see this play out in how Ephesians lifts up marriage as a way of understanding Christ's relationship with the church (Ephesians 5) whereas Paul earlier wrote in 1 Corinthians 7:7 that he wished everyone were still single (like him) since Christ is coming again soon.

None of these differences in and of themselves are enough to say that someone else wrote the letter using Paul's name, but in aggregate they persuade many scholars that someone who knew Paul well wrote this in his name at a later date. It should be noted, however, that in the ancient world it would not have been surprising to have someone write a letter in another's name [ERD]. In fact, they probably would have known it was written by someone else. If this letter was written by someone later in Paul's name, the early church was aware of it and chose it to be included in the New Testament anyway based on its impact in the churches at the time.

Regardless of authorship, we can infer a few contextual clues by reading the letter. The heavy emphasis on the role of Gentile Christians suggests that they needed a boost of hope and purpose – a kind of pep talk. Most likely this was as a result of competing ideas from the religious practices of the surrounding cultures, though persecution is also possible. The best clue we have for this comes from reading Revelation 2:1-7 (see above) and Ephesians 6:

> *For our struggle is not against flesh and blood, but against the rulers, against the authorities, against the powers of this dark world and against the spiritual forces of evil in the heavenly realms. – Ephesians 6:12 (NIV)*

In some respects, the less specific nature of Ephesians makes it easier for us to see ourselves in it. This letter, written to several churches, could easily be written to our church today.

Tips for Reading

As with any reading of Scripture, it can be useful to apply the Observation, Interpretation, Application technique. As you read, make Observations by noting what's actually said. If you are reading a familiar passage, you might want to slow down and write down what you see so you eye doesn't just skip over it. Once you have noted what is said, try to Interpret why it was written that way. Finally, ask what Application there might be to your life.

Another way to engage with the text of Ephesians is to note the two major sections. For the first three chapters, the author talks about the cosmic, all-encompassing nature of Jesus Christ. Chapter one mentions that we were chosen "before the creation of the world" (NIV). Chapter two describes how everything is knitted together into a "holy temple in the Lord" (NIV). Chapter three talks about taking the good news of Jesus Christ to "the rulers and authorities in the heavenly realms" (NIV). The "Amen" at the end of chapter three marks a turning point where the letter starts addressing the more earthly concerns. Chapter four starts off by a challenge to "live a life worthy of the calling you have received" (NIV). Chapters five and six address how we speak to each other, how we relate in marriage, how we relate in employment, and how we relate in families.

Similarly, there is a common theme of "before" and "after." For example, Ephesians 5:8 says, "For you were once darkness, but now you are light in the Lord" (NIV). As you read this letter, see where the author highlights the impact and change that is expected once faith has taken root in a person's life.

You can also see a vast array of images used to describe the church. The church is compared to a body, a house, an army, little children, a family, a bride, and even a prisoner. As these images are used in the letter, think through the image and see if it has any relevance for you personally or for your church.

Finally, the letter to the Ephesians can be seen as a birds-eye-view of God's overall story. Right at the start this letter acknowledges that God has had a plan from the beginning of time. That story finds its climax in Jesus, but it's still playing out through many generations.

GOING DEEPER

- What parallels and differences do you see between Ephesus and where you live?
- Why do you think God did such amazing miracles in Ephesus but not in other places?
- What do you hope to get out of this Bible study? Is there any particular area of life in which you hope to hear from the Holy Spirit?

Using This Bible Study With a Small Group or Class

This Bible study was originally created as a six-week class at the First Presbyterian Church of Littleton, Colorado. Since each chapter is split into two main sections, it is very simple to expand the schedule to 12 weeks. Considering the amount of background material, it is also possible to have a dedicated introduction. Below are some suggested schedules depending on your needs.

There are also short (2-3 minute) introduction videos for each chapter available for streaming or download at my website: **www.codysandahl.com/ephesians.**

6-8 Weeks	12-14 Weeks
(Optional) Background and Introduction	(Optional) Background and Introduction
Week 1: Ephesians 1	Week 1: Ephesians 1:1-14
Week 2: Ephesians 2	Week 2: Ephesians 1:15-23
Week 3: Ephesians 3	Week 3: Ephesians 2:1-10
Week 4: Ephesians 4	Week 4: Ephesians 2:11-22
Week 5: Ephesians 5	Week 5: Ephesians 3:1-13
Week 6: Ephesians 6	Week 6: Ephesians 3:14-21
(Optional) Summary and Major Take-Aways	Week 7: Ephesians 4:1-16
	Week 8: Ephesians 4:17-32
	Week 9: Ephesians 5:1-20
	Week 10: Ephesians 5:21-33
	Week 11: Ephesians 6:1-9
	Week 12: Ephesians 6:10-24
	(Optional) Summary and Major Take-Aways

References and Abbreviations

[NIV] THE HOLY BIBLE, NEW INTERNATIONAL VERSION®, NIV® Copyright © 1973, 1978, 1984, 2011 by Biblica, Inc.® Used by permission. All rights reserved worldwide.

[EAS] Easton, Matthew George. *Illustrated Bible Dictionary, Third Edition.* 1897.

[ERD] Freedman, David Noel, Allen C. Myers, and Astrid B. Beck, ed. *Eerdman's Dictionary of the Bible.* Grand Rapids: Eerdmans. 2000.

[ISBE] Bromiley, Geoffrey W., ed. *International Standard Bible Encyclopedia.* Eerdmans. 1986.

[DBI] Ryken, Leland, James C. Wilhoit, and Tremper Longman III, ed. *Dictionary of Biblical Imagery.* Downers Grove: InterVarsity Press. 1998.

[KIT] Kittel, Gerhard. *Theological Dictionary of the New Testament, Volume 5.* Eerdmans. 1984.

[ARCH] *Archaeological Study Bible.* Grand Rapids: Zondervan. 2005.

[MOU] Mounce, William D. *Mounce's Complete Expository Dictionary of Old and New Testament Words.* Grand Rapids: Zondervan. 2006.

[APOL] *Apologetics Study Bible.* Nashville: Holman. 2007.

[JNTC] Stern, David H. *Jewish New Testament Commentary.* Clarksville: Jewish. 1989.

[WORD] Lincoln, Andrew. *Word Biblical Commentary, Volume 42: Ephesians.* Grand Rapids:Zondervan. 2014.

[VINE] Vine, W.E. *Vine's Complete Expository Dictionary of Old and New Testament Words.* Thomas Nelson. 1996.

[IVP] Keener, Craig S. *InterVarsity Press Bible Background Commentary: The New Testament.* Downers Grove: InterVarsity. 2014.

[REF] *Reformation Study Bible.* Ligonier. 2005.

[GLOB] *Global Study Bible.* Crossway. 2012.

[VINC] Vincent, Marvin R. Word Studies in the New Testament.

[ACC] Edwards, Mark J., ed. *Ancient Christian Commentary on Scripture, Volume 8: Galatians, Ephesians, Philippians.* IVP Academic. 2006.

[WEB1] Rutledge, Pamela B. https://www.psychologytoday.com/blog/positively-media/201101/the-psychological-power-storytelling

[WEB2] Greer, Ronald J. http://www.heavenlydove.com/firstchapter.asp?mode=view&index=1453

[WEB3] Mark, Joshua J. http://www.ancient.eu/socrates/

[WEB4] Park, Chris. http://www.lancaster.ac.uk/staff/gyaccp/geography%20and%20religion.pdf

[WEB5] http://www.pewforum.org/2011/12/19/global-christianity-exec/

[WEB6] Lull, David J. http://www.ncccusa.org/newbtu/lullking.html

[WEB7] http://www.ushistory.org/us/27f.asp

[WEB8] Robinson, B.A. http://www.religioustolerance.org/chr_slav4.htm

[WEB9] Weird, Tom. http://content.usatoday.com/communities/gameon/post/2009/02/63418703/1#.Vzyp55ErKhc

www.ingramcontent.com/pod-product-compliance
Lightning Source LLC
Chambersburg PA
CBHW071411040426
42444CB00009B/2205